1001 Questions

To Help Flesh out Your Character

- -

CHRISTINA ESCAMILLA

Christina Escamilla
Publishing

Christina Escamilla Publishing | **www.christinaescamilla.com**

INTRODUCTION

How do you create a human being from nothing? This question is at the forefront of fiction writing, as without a solid character foundation, your book is merely words on a page rather than a fully immersive world. From the protagonists of the story to the background players, each character in your great work of literature must have a fully constructed frame for you to build upon.

Characters that have a strong framework will begin to cast shadows as the plot continues. They become so real that the audience becomes trapped; the suspension of disbelief creates a shell in which the reader is separated from their own reality. As a writer, this is what you want. You want the book to haunt the reader years after they have put it down.

And it all starts with the characters you create.

This guide has one definitive purpose – to give you food for thought when crafting your characters. There are four sections in total: Background, Mind, Body, and Soul. The background section helps you to create the base framework, the character's full back story. The next section is devoted entirely to your character's underlining motivations and personality traits. The body segment is to help give visual representation to your character through the power of your writing. The soul section is a compilation of character scenarios that will give you a better sense of how your character might respond to any given situation. Finally, the extra sections are to help you when it comes to characters that may not fit into mainstream fiction writing.

Keep in mind that the following guides are written in full question format in order to encourage you to come up with an answer without over-thinking. This way, you are actively participating in the creation process even when answering simple questions.

Although, you obviously do not have to complete the whole guide for your character, the more of the guideline you utilize the more the character becomes real to you.

It is also important to consider using the guideline for each character in your novel, not just the main players. The more characters you understand, the more realistic it is when your primary characters interact with them.

I hope this guide gives you a stepping point to polish up your characters!

Happy Writing,

Christina

Table of Contents

BACKGROUND

The character background is by far one of the most easily forgotten aspects of character design, though it has a large effect on how your character interacts with others around them, and how they came to be who they are today. A flat character can, for example, be abandoned on a tropical island the same as a complex one. Canonically, you could have them build a raft, but without understanding their background you have no idea how logical this is for them. Are they coming from the middle of a hot, desert town or are they coming from a small lake village where boating is common place? If it's the former, then it simply would not make sense for them to easily construct something that would float from only the materials available on the island.

All that is important background information you need to keep in mind before starting on your prose.

The Basics

To construct your own character, let's start with the basics of their background:

1.   What is your character's full name?

2. And how do you pronounce that?
3. What's the meaning of the name?
4. Do they have a specific nickname, or perhaps an alias, maiden name, etc.?
5. Where did the nickname (etc.) come from?
6. Do they have another special nickname by their spouse or close friend?
7. What is it?
8. Where did the nickname come from?
9. How old is the character?
10. When is their date of birth?
11. That means their zodiac sign is?
12. Which makes them how old?
13. What is their biological gender?
14. What is their identifiable gender?
15. Sexual Orientation?
16. How many sexual partners have they had?
17. What are the names of their past partners?
18. What languages do they know?
19. Can they write well?
20. Can they read well?
21. What is their potential IQ?
22. Compared to others, would their intellect be considered average, high, or poor?
23. What is their date of death?
24. How old will they be when they die?
25. What will be their manner of death?

Biographical Information

Your character's upbringing is paramount to how they would

react to certain situations as an adult, or even as a young child.
Let's work on creating a background that will give you more insight,
shall we?

26. Do they have biological, adoptive, or other type of parental units?
27. Are they alive?
28. When did they die?
29. Where do they live now?
30. What are their names and ages?
31. How many siblings do they have?
32. What are their names and ages?
33. Compared to their siblings, what place are they? E.g. middle child, youngest, only child, etc.
34. Any nephews, nieces, aunts, uncles, or other family members of note?
35. What are their names and ages?
36. Are there any known ancestors?
37. Does the family have specific enemies?
38. What about allies?
39. Does your character still live with any family member?
40. What is your character's place of birth?
41. Do they have a family symbol? E.g. crest, shield, etc.
42. What is their ethnic background?
43. Where do they live now?
44. What is the environment like?

45. What was the parent's (or guardians) occupation as your character grew up?
46. Has your character ever broken the law?
47. What was it?
48. How old were they?
49. What kind of education did they have?
50. What kind of grades did they get?
51. What was their economic situation?
52. What is your character's economic class now?
53. How much wealth do they have?
54. What are their debts?
55. What kind of income does their primary job generate?
56. What is your character's current education status?
57. What was/is their major?
58. What was/is their grades?
59. Do they receive any kind of special training?
60. What was it?
61. Is your character currently in any association? E.g. a guild or club.
62. What is your character's current occupation?
63. What kind of experience did they have?
64. How did they get the job?
65. How long have they been working there?
66. What is your character's work schedule like?
67. What is their current criminal record?
68. What were the crimes?
69. What is your character's marital status?
70. What is their spouse's name?
71. Do they have a boyfriend/girlfriend?

72. Do they have any children?
73. What are their names?
74. Does your character have any grandchildren?
75. What are their names?

THE MIND

A mind is a terrible thing to waste, as the saying goes. For your character – the last thing you should do is give them a fairly decent background, but then fail to give them any kind of personality. Remember, a Mary Sue or Gary Sue (male and female characters that are considered 'perfect') often become such because the writer creates a cardboard brain. You want a character that is personable, and while they may certainly be flawed, they should still have complex aspects that don't shift towards either scale of black or white. Think about your own day-to-day life. Is your daily choices based entirely on the traditional notion of 'good' and 'evil' or are you simply making second-to-second choices based on the all of the information available to you. The best villains, despite their characterization as evil, really believe that they are engaging in the best course of action.

Keep this in mind as you move through this section.

Personality Traits

Your character will have many personality traits. At times, they may be angry or sad; sometimes they may be downright depressed. The surge of emotions that changes based on any given circumstances is what makes us human. However, each individual may be more resilient or more prone to anger. It's up to you to discover these nuances.

76. What is the personality type of your character?

77. How good are they at interacting in social situations?
78. Are they good with people?
79. What are some of your character's favorite things?
80. Favorite color?
81. Food?
82. Musical Genre?
83. Do they have a motto they live by?
84. What is it?
85. Does the character have a special talent?
86. What are their hobbies?
87. Are they easily bored?
88. Do they have any known quirks?
89. Do they prefer the quiet or do they hate the silence?
90. Does your character have any mementos that are special to them?
91. What are they?
92. What experiences do they like the least? E.g. going to the dentists, fighting off invaders, etc.
93. Do they have any fears?
94. What role does your character take in a group? E.g. leader, rebel, outcast, follower, etc.
95. In a group setting, what would they most likely contribute? E.g. good at generating ideas, delegation, analysis, etc.
96. How good is your character at cooperating?
97. What kind of thinker are they? E.g. idealist, realist, optimist, etc.

98. What annoys your character?
99. What does your character do when they are annoyed?
100. When they are angry?
101. Are they easily angered?
102. Are they sad often?
103. What do they do when they are sad?
104. What are their main strengths?
105. What are their main weaknesses?
106. Does your character have any immediate goals?
107. Do they have any long-term goals?
108. Is your character self-serving or are they more prone to be self-sacrificing?
109. Is your character a dreamer or more of a realist?
110. What kind of personality flaws does your character have?
111. How reliable is your character's memory?
112. What is their earliest memory?
113. What is their fondest memory?
114. What is their most embarrassing moment?
115. What is your character's biggest failure?
116. What is their biggest regret?
117. What is their greatest achievement?
118. Are they self-confident or self-depreciating?
119. Does your character have any triggers related to past traumas?
120. What was the trauma?
121. What is their primary method to calm down?
122. What kind of humor does your character have?
123. Is your character good at keeping secrets?

124. Is your character prone to gossip?
125. Does your character have messy or neat handwriting?

Guiding Motivations

Now we are in the thick of it. The nitty gritty of why your character does what they do. I am not just referring to the main plot arc your character falls into, but what guides them for every action they take: from the people they fall for to the things they fight for. Let's figure it out together.

126. In a social group, are they submissive or dominate?
127. Were they ever bullied or teased when they were younger?
128. By whom?
129. Are they bullied or teased now?
130. By whom?
131. Does your character get along well with their parents or guardians?
132. What are the issues?
133. What about their siblings?
134. What are the issues?
135. Does your character have a lot of friends?
136. Do they have a lot of romantic partners?
137. Did they ever suffer a bad breakup?
138. Who did it involve?
139. What happened?
140. Do they have any jealous lovers?

141. Does their family have a reputation outside of the home?
142. What is the religion of the family?
143. Is their religion important for the family?
144. What is your character's religion?
145. How important is religion for your character?
146. Does your character have a specific moral code that is unique and outside of religion? I.e. a personal code of ethics.
147. What is the family's political affiliation?
148. Is politics important for your character's family?
149. What is your character's political affiliation?
150. Is politics important for your character?
151. What is your character's main reputation among their family?
152. Among their friends?
153. Among society at large?
154. Compared to the common social hierarchy, what is their social status?
155. Was your character active in the community when they were younger?
156. What did they do?
157. Are they active now?
158. What do they do?
159. Does your character have any bad memories as a child?
160. What about happy ones?
161. Does your character have any manias? I.e. anything they are obsessed with.
162. What are they?

163. Are they very inept at something?
164. What is it?
165. Does your character have any taboos?
166. What are they?
167. Does your character have any secrets?
168. What are they?
169. Does your character have any specific enemies?
170. Who are they?
171. What about rivals?
172. Who are they?
173. Is your character in poor health or have primary medical complaints?
174. Is your character of sound mine?
175. No mental health concerns?

THE BODY

It's easy to simply chalk your character up to: male standing 6ft 2, with black hair and brown eyes. However, there are billions of people in the world that would fit this exact description. Simply saying that your character has black hair does not indicate if it's thinning, if it's long, short, brittle, curly, etc. You picture the character clearly in your head, but you need to ensure that your audience does too. Vague descriptors will only give your audience a general sense of what your character may look like. At times, this can be enough. However, giving yourself a full and concise written description can make it easier to draw back to as you move through your novel. Moreover, you can also use it as a reference if you decide to get art of your character made or you need to give your cover designer something to work with if you are self-publishing.

Primary Visuals

Let's start by outlining the main graphic elements, the first thing that the audience will visualize when they are first introduced to the character.

176. What is their skin color?
177. How tall is the character?
178. In comparison to others in the piece, is this height considered short, medium, or average?
179. Do they have long legs or arms?

180. Is your character right-handed, left-handed, or ambidextrous?

181. Is their body type Ectomorph (slim), Mesomorph (muscular), or Endomorph (more curvy)?

182. Do they have a small, medium, or large frame?

183. What kind of overall shape do they have? E.g. more triangular, pear-shaped, hourglass, round, etc.

184. How much body fat do they have?

185. What about muscle?

186. What kind of face shape does the character have? E.g. oval, round, rectangular, heart, etc.

187. Does your character have a low, average, or high forehead?

188. Do they have distinguishing features to their forehead such as wrinkles, widow's peak, sloped, etc?

189. What kind of skin do they have? E.g. oily, dry, sensitive, flaky, etc.

190. Does your character have flat, curved, or arched eyebrows?

191. Compared to their eyes, does your character have eyebrows that are high or low?

192. Do they have long lashes, short, or average?

193. What color eyes do they have?

194. Are their eyes closer together or wider apart?

195. What type of nose shape do they have? E.g. hawk-nosed, hooked, Greek, pointy, fleshy, etc.

196. What does their mouth look like? I.e. would the top lip be wider than the bottom, or are both lips equally full?
197. In comparison to their mouth, how big are their teeth?
198. Do they have small, large or average sized hands?
199. What about finger length?
200. Are they missing any appendages? E.g. arm, leg, fingers, etc.

Physical Attributes

Now that we have the main body fleshed out, it's time to get more technical. Although, many of these characteristics may not make it into the final prose, these descriptions will help polish off some of the rough edges that are often left behind.

201. Does your character look much younger or older than they are biologically?
202. Are they considered traditionally attractive?
203. In what way?
204. Are they considered traditionally ugly?
205. In what way?
206. Do they look healthy and in good shape?
207. Why/Why not?
208. What is their most predominate feature?
209. Is your character's weight often fluctuating?
210. What is their current weight?
211. What are their clothing measurements?
212. What is their shoe size?

213. Compared to others, do they have big or small feet?
214. What kind of gait does your character have?
215. When standing, what kind of stance do they naturally fall into?
216. Do they utilize common gestures when speaking? E.g. biting their lip, playing with their clothes, etc.
217. Is your character often expressive when speaking?
218. What common expressions do they display? i.e. facial expressions or speaking with hands.
219. Do they display any strange mannerisms?
220. What are they?
221. How long is the character's hair?
222. What color is it?
223. How is it styled?
224. Is their hair thick, thin, or average?
225. Do they have facial hair?
226. If so, how is their facial hair styled?
227. Is the color of their facial hair different than the hair on their head?
228. What about body hair?
229. Is their body hair similar to skin tone?
230. Do they have an accent?
231. Is it common to the region or foreign?
232. What kind of voice pitch do they have?
233. What is their quality of voice? E.g. breathy or croaky?
234. Compared to others, would their voice be considered distinctive?

235. Are any of their senses noticeably better than the others?

236. What about worse?

237. Does your character have a natural noticeable smell?

238. Is it good or bad?

239. What is the smell often described as?

240. Do they have chipped, crooked, or otherwise damaged teeth?

241. Do any of these damages require the need of corrections? I.e false teeth or braces?

242. Do they have good or poor vision?

243. Does poor vision require corrections? I.e. contact lenses or glasses?

244. Do they have long fingernails or short?

245. What is the condition of their fingernails? i.e. are they chewed or meticulously manicured?

246. Are their hands noticeable in any way? i.e. calloused or claw-like?

247. Does your character have any tattoos?

248. What about scars or birthmarks?

249. Any other distinguishing features?

250. What are they?

Personality & Style

Characters in TV shows and movies can often be identifiable based off their clothing alone. Superman dons his red and blue suit while Jason Voorhees puts on his creepy hockey mask. What about the things that they like? Such as the pets that they have or the book they are most likely to pick up? As writers, clothing and personal style choices aren't always necessary to include, and thus, many of us don't bother with visualizing this aspect of the character at all. However, we need to keep these selections in mind because it reveals a great deal about personality.

251. What kind of style of clothing does your character wear?
252. Where do these clothes usually come from? E.g. from a high end store, the character makes them, the character is donated them, etc.
253. Does your character dress themselves?
254. Why not?
255. Compared to society at large, is their clothing selection considered fashionable?
256. What kind of mode of dress do they have? I.e. how do they wear their clothes?
257. What kind of grooming habits do they have? I.e. kept meticulously clean or in a usual state of messiness?
258. Do they put a lot of foresight into what they wear each day?
259. What kind of top might your character wear?
260. Bottoms?
261. Shoes?
262. Would they be prone to wearing hats?
263. What kind?
264. Does the character wear makeup?
265. How much makeup do they put on?

266. Is it more natural or more towards the dramatic side?
267. Do they wear head accessories? E.g. hair accessories, nose rings, earrings, etc.
268. What kind?
269. Do they often have clothing accessories? E.g. scarf, necklaces, bracelet, etc.?
270. Compared to everyone else, do they have any unusual clothing accessories?
271. Do they carry any equipment on them?
272. What about trinkets or mementos?
273. What kind of home do they have? E.g. mansion, small house, mud hut, tree house, etc.
274. Is it well-kept?
275. Is this where they chose to live or is it the product of circumstance?
276. Where would they choose to live?
277. What is their favorite color?
278. Why?
279. What is your character's favorite animal?
280. Do they have any pets?
281. Are the pets well kept? E.g. the animal is mistreated, it is spoiled, etc.
282. Are they prone to believing in fairytales, myths, urban legends, or other unverifiable stories?
283. What is their favorite fairytale, myth, etc.?
284. What is their favorite mythological creature?
285. Are they well read?
286. What is their favorite book genre?
287. What is their favorite book?

288. Do they watch a lot of movies or TV shows?
289. What is their favorite movie?
290. What is their favorite TV show?
291. Do they play any instruments?
292. Which one?
293. Can they sing?
294. What is their favorite song?
295. What is their favorite food?
296. Drink?
297. What is their favorite place? E.g. their bedroom, the tree at the house they grew up, Paris, London, etc.
298. Do they play any sports?
299. What is their favorite sport?
300. What is their favorite quote?

THE SOUL

You now have a believable character to work with. Before, or as, you write your novel it is good practice to place your character in a variety of different situations, even outside the scope of your genre. Doing so will allow you to understand how your character will react to any given situation. The more you understand what their reactions and actions might be the better your story will flow as you begin to place your character into the actual plot of the novel.

Character Prompts

301. Your character is in the *Harry Potter* world and is sorted by the sorting hat. What house are they placed in?

302. Your character catches a magic wish fish in an enchanted stream. The fish pleads to be thrown back. Do they throw the fish back or make a wish?

303. If they choose to make a wish, what is one thing they wish for?

304. Your character stumbles across a magic lamp that doesn't give wishes – it adds ten yours to your life each time you rub it. However, the catch is that it will take life away from someone else. Does your character use it anyway?

305. If so, do they use it to become immortal or do they have a set age in mind?

306. What is the age?

307. Your character and their sibling are very sick and need special medicine. The only problem is that there is only enough for one person. Who gets it?

308. What if it was a best friend that was sick?

309. What about their parents or guardians?

310. Their enemy?

311. Your character is in charge of a sinking ship and there are not enough lifeboats for everyone. How does your character delegate who gets to use them and who must stay on board?

312. What do they decide?

313. On a different ship, what role would they play? E.g. captain, first mate, a passenger, regular crew mate, etc.

314. Your character is stranded on a deserted island. They have enough wood to try and build a raft in order to swim to safety or enough wood for a small camp where they can wait to be rescued. Which do they do?

315. On that deserted island your character has three additional items that do not help with survival, but can help with boredom. What are those items?

316. On the island your character comes across a group of natives that are sacrificing a victim to the God Ba'lammrii. Spotting your character, they carry them off and give them a choice: aid in the next sacrifice or become the sacrifice. What do they choose to do?

317. Your character is ordering coffee at their favorite shop. They have enough for their drink and a special treat, but not enough for a decent tip. Do they pick something for a special treat anyway or do they use the remainder to tip the barista?

318. At the local coffee shop, your character notices that the barista is very attractive. Even better, the barista seems to be equally interested. How do they make their move?

319. At the grocery store your character is behind a very angry woman in line. She is cursing and screaming at the cashier because of a mispriced item. Your character knows it is not the fault of the cashier. Do they choose to intervene or ignore the angry woman?

320. While getting gas at a convenience store your character sees someone stealing a couple of items, shoving the merchandize under their thick coat. Do they alert the cashier, or ignore the theft?

321. In the same scenario, suppose your character previously saw the thief before and know that they are homeless. Further, the items they are stealing are basic necessities, such as food or sanitary products. What would they choose to do then?

322. Your character suddenly finds their house on fire. What three items do they take with them when escaping?

323. Suppose in that burning house, aside from your character, there is also their mother, the love of

their life, and a beloved pet. Who do they choose to save first?

324. Who do they save last?

325. After eating tainted tacos your character suddenly finds themselves waking up as the opposite gender. What is the first thing that they do?

326. Your character suddenly finds themselves under the glamour of a strange curse. They have suddenly become an animal for no apparent reason whatsoever. What is the animal they are turned into?

327. What is the foremost place they look in an effort to discover why they have been cursed in the first place?

328. Your character is five years old again and eating an ice cream cone in the hot summer sun. Unfortunately, a bully also chances by and steals it from them. What do they do?

329. Your character is still five years old and a scary monster is hidden inside their closet. Although, they yell for someone to help as loud as they can it seems no help is coming. Do they wait or take matters into their own hands?

330. While taking a leisurely stroll one day, your character stumbles across a strange object in the middle of the forest. Upon closer inspection they realize that it is a crashed flying saucer! Do they inspect the aircraft or get out of dodge?

331. Your character is in a daring sword fight where they are mortally wounded. They are going to die soon, without question. Do they ask for their death to be quick or wait it out?

332. Your lonely character is alone in their bedroom wishing upon a star that they could have a friend. Their wish is granted and a new friend pops into their room. What might this friend be like?

333. Your character picks up a strange red and white ball. Out of it, their very own Pokémon is unleashed. Which one is it?

334. Your character is walking past an alley when a little kitten chances by. Your character instinctively reaches out and picks the little ball of fluff up. The kitten reacts by biting them on the hand. How does your character respond?

335. Your character is listening to a song on the radio. It speaks to them on a deeply personal level. What are the lyrics to that song?

336. Your character finds themselves alone in the bedroom of their love interest. The love interested they might just get lucky with. Who makes the first move?

337. If it's your character, how do they go about initiating the act?

338. Your character is marrying the love of their life and is able to write their own vows. What are they?

339. Your character's rival crashes that very wedding and loudly objects, saying that they still love the groom/bride. How does your character react?

340. Your character has found out that they've been cheated on. Their partner swears that it will never happen again. Does your character choose to believe them or get revenge anyway?

341. Your character is invited to a dinner party by five historical figures. Who are they?

342. When they get there, what is their beginning topic of choice?

343. Your character decides to become a rebel against traditional society. They attend a protest to show their support. What are they protesting?

344. At the protest, your character is holding up a sign they made themselves. What does it say?

345. Your character awakes from a terrifying, blood-draining nightmare. What does it entail?

346. While travelling across a desert plain, your character suddenly runs out of water. They can try to look for some, potentially getting lost along the way, or they can stay and wait for rescue which may also prove to be problematic. What do they do?

347. Your character is attending college for the first time. Excitedly, they get to choose three extra credit courses. What do they pick?

348. Your character has been sent to the guild of assassins to study the ways of death. What do

they excel in? E.g. poisons, stealth, knife throwing, etc.

349. Your character stumbles across an ornate box that is locked up tightly. Without having any kind of knowledge what the box contains, would your character open it?

350. If they do, what might the character find inside?

351. Your character is all alone in the house during a rainstorm. Against the brightness of lightening, they swear they see something lurking outside the window. Do they go and investigate or wait for the best?

352. If they choose to investigate, suppose they go outside and don't find anything. However, when they come back inside they see a familiar person sitting at the dinner table. Who is it?

353. What is it that they want?

354. One day while opening the mail, your character finds that they have won a free cruise to a place they've always wanted to go! However, it corresponds with a very important engagement that they promised they would attend. Which event do they choose?

355. Your character has suddenly become poor and is living off of the streets. Although, destitute they have not given up hope. What is the first thing they might try to improve their current situation?

356. While at a bar, a very loud and drunk individual begins to sling insults towards your character. How might they respond?

357.   One night, a mysterious man approaches your character. Hearing of their widely known skills the stranger ask your character to kill a specific target in exchange for a very large sum of money as a reward for the deadly deed. What sort of skills does your character possess?

358.   As it turns out, that target happens to be someone very close to your character. What would your character decide to do?

359.   While at a film premiere your character sees their favorite celebrity chance by. It just so happens that they are holding a picture of that very celebrity and a sharpie. However, after asking for an autograph not only is your character rudely turned down, but they are also pushed away. What does your character do in response to the slight?

360.   Perhaps the opposite is true. The celebrity is so entranced by your character that they ask them to run away together and lead a new life of luxury. What does your character say to the proposal?

361.   While walking into the recesses of a busy crowded subway, your character sees a familiar face – the murderer of their parents or guardians. Since it happened when they were younger, the murderer obviously doesn't recognize them. Does your character seek after revenge, warn the police, or simply let the murderer walk on by?

362. If they choose the former, how do they go about seeking their revenge?

363. Your character finds themselves arrested for a crime that they did not commit. How do they go about seeking justice for themselves?

364. Your character is arrested, but they did commit the crime. Alarmingly, there is overwhelming proof of their guilt. What have they been accused of?

365. While speeding down the street at an alarming rate your character hears a loud thump under their car. When they stop and step outside, they see they have run over a dog. Thankfully, the dog is alive, but needs medical attention pronto. Your character is in a rush to get to a very important event. What do they decide to do?

366. What if it was a person they hit?

367. Suppose that they did hit the person and getting the poor soul help would also get your character in serious trouble. What do they choose to do then?

368. Your character has found a nifty time machine that actually works! There is just enough fuel for only a one-way trip. They can choose to visit a place in history they have always been fascinated by and live out their days there, or they can choose to go back to a former time in their own life and start over. Which do they decide to do?

369. If they choose to start over, what age do they decide to start at?

370. If they choose to go back to a different time entirely, what period in history do they choose?

371. After a heavy snowstorm, your character goes outside to collect more wood. Once there, they see strange tracks on the ground made by no animal they have ever seen before. Do they decide to follow the tracks and investigate?

372. If so, what might they find if they follow the tracks to the unusual creature itself?

373. Oh no! It seems that a surprise rain has made its way over your character's romantic picnic. How might your character try and salvage the rest of their date?

374. Your character finds themselves trapped in the home of a serial killer. Not only are they chained up in a cell, but there are other captives here too. Would your character try to work together to escape or would they try to escape first then send help after?

375. Suppose that escaping themselves would mean certain death for the other captors while attempting to work together would potentially mean death for everyone if they are found. What does your character choose then?

376. After weeks of being lost at sea your character finally sees a small island. However, on that island are human skeletons hanging in trees. They have managed to last this long merely drifting on

their raft, but there might be food and shelter on the island! Does your character decide to land?

377. While pirating a ship, your character stumbles across a group of female/male sirens. Their voices are melodic and their appearance is very seductive. It's been a very long time since they have been in the company of anyone outside their small, unappealing crew. Will your character take the bait?

378. Today is your character's birthday! How might they spend the day celebrating?

379. Today is your character's death day. Their last day on Earth. How might they spend the day before they pass?

380. Your character awakes one day to find themselves trapped in a strange room. They are shackled by both the legs and arms, but there is just enough leverage to move their hands to the key in front of them. However, above the key there is a sign that reads, "Take this key and live, but someone else will die." Do they take the key anyway?

381. Suppose your character chooses to take the key and they hear a familiar scream, before silence. They realize with horror that they have just killed the love of their life. Although, they are now free a small window in the ceiling is opened and a loaded gun drops down. Will your character choose a life without their love or a chance to meet them on the other side?

382. Your character is a teenager and has just been taken to a theme park where they have free reign with all of their friends. What ride do they go straight for?

383. While at that same theme park your character's friend dares them to do something really dangerous, like ride the rollercoaster without buckling or sneak into a restricted area. Will your character give in to the peer pressure or refuse?

384. While making their way to the bathroom at a restaurant, your character happens across the kitchens instead. Curiously, they decide to peak through and are horrified to see that the main ingredient in the soup is people! Do they warn the other patrons, risking potential retaliation, or simply run out of there?

385. Your character is signed up for a very intensive cross country marathon. Aside from running, what method does your character use to get into shape?

386. Sword in hand, your character is about to face an ogre. Their one weak spot happens to be their heart, which makes the task difficult seeing as they stand at over twelve feet tall. Is your character going to come out victorious, or will their skull join the others that adorn the belt the ogre wears?

387. If your character will no doubt be victorious, other than swordplay, how will that victory be fostered in?

388. How embarrassing! Your character has been caught with their pants down, literally. What have they been caught doing?

389. Your character suddenly finds themselves in a foreign city where they do not speak the language. On top of this, they are utterly lost and their home is half way across the world. How do they fair in this strange predicament?

390. Your character decides to launch a crowd funding campaign in order to fund their pet project. What is that project?

391. How successful do you think your character would be with this campaign?

392. Congrats! Your character has just earned their first badge in their wilderness troupe. What is it they have earned?

393. Your character stumbles across an injured bear cub. Do they decide to help the poor animal or move on in fear that its mother might be lurking nearby?

394. Your character is witness to a crime happening in real time. Your character knows that it will likely end with harm coming to the victim. Do they step in or go on about their business?

395. While hanging out with their best friends, your character hears one of them make a very offensive joke. The others join in, but it does not sit well

with your character. Do they join in the laughter anyway or speak up?

396. Your character is offered a seat on a high council where they are offered a chance to influence the decisions of the king. Up for debate: whether or not to go to war with an opposing fraction. Troops are severally limited. Half of the council wants to keep the troops at home for defensive purposes while the other half wants to send the troops out in an offensive strike. What is it that your character suggests?

397. Later, the kingdom must also deal with an equally pressing issue: focus on harvesting the crops as the countryside has been hit with a devastating famine, keeping the peace from an incoming invasion, or abandoning all hope and starting a new kingdom elsewhere. What does your character suggest?

398. Your character happens across an ancient object of extraordinary power. They recognize this power as one that is often affiliated with evil and know it to be very dangerous. Your character has a chance to destroy the artifact, but do they decide to use its power instead?

399. After a long and tedious battle, your character's sworn enemy is now yielding to you on their hands and knees. Do they accept their white flag offer and take the enemy prisoner as an act of

mercy or do they decide to take their enemy's life instead?

400. Your character has just been accepted to the League of Superheroes. What is their special power?

401. What might their costume look like?

402. Your character and their best friend are members of a supernatural agency. During one investigation they find a portal to hell has been opened, releasing countless demons upon the Earth. In order to close it a sacrifice must be made. Your character sees their friend begin to run towards the swirling circle of energy. What does your character decide to do?

403. After a painful breakup, your character decides that the best course of action to take is a night of gluttonous binge eating. What is it they decide to feast on?

404. Several years ago, your character's best friend was shot and killed by a mugger. More recently, your character happens across the path of that very same mugger, but they are living a quiet life with a family of their own. Does your character take any action against them?

405. Your character is a world famous explorer who often gets rich off of their excursions because of the many priceless treasures they bring back. During one such excursion they happen across a treasure that is worth more than anything they've stumbled on before. As it turns out, the treasure is a sacred object from a nearby village. Does your character decide to take it anyway?

406. It seems your character has lost their memory, and does not recall who they or anyone else is. How do they deal with the change?

407. Your character decides to write a book that they hope will become a bestseller. What is the title of the book?

408. What is the genre?

409. What is the summary?

410. Your character is locked inside a prison with only a barred window looking to the outside world. Looking out of it, they see that they are on the highest point of a mountain. How do they make their escape?

411. While visiting a rather seedy motel your character hears screams from the room on the opposite end of the hall. Do they decide to investigate for themselves, presumably to save whoever is screaming, or do they run off and tell hotel management instead?

412. While browsing the internet your character comes across a website that is accidentally selling items at an extremely low price. They are aware that this is obviously a glitch in the system, but also know that if they put in their order, there is a good chance they can get the items at 90% off the regular value. What does your character decide to do?

413. The zombie apocalypse has just hit. Staying in your character's current location would mean a swarm of hungry zombies at their doorstep. Thus, they know they must act fast. What would their escape plan be?

414. Sadly, your character's child has been turned into a zombie. What does your character do in response?

415. It's the harshest winter your character has ever known. Disease is beginning to run rampant and people are dropping like flies. Not to mention, starvation is a very real threat as the food has run out for a few days now. Spring is still two months away. One of the townspeople has suggested eating the dead for survival. Where does your character stand on the issue?

416. After an exceptionally heroic deed, your character has been taken to Mt. Olympus to be one of the new deities. What is your character the God/Goddess of?

417. Your character finds out that they have a very special talent. Whatever it is that they paint will come to life. How do they put this strange artistic talent to use?

418. After getting the mail one day, your character finds out that they've been sent a particularly threatening letter. Your character has some idea who sent the letter but have no real proof. What do they do?

419. Your character has been spent an anonymous donation of one million dollars. How do they spend the money?

420. Down on their luck and extremely hungry, your character is overjoyed when a truck-full of food ends up on their doorstep out of the blue. They have enough ingredients to craft whatever they want. What is the first meal they decide to make?

421. Oddly enough, your character finds out that the food has been stolen from the local food bank. Not only is your character confused as to why it was sent to them, but after two weeks of feasting like a king, the food is all gone. What will your character do now?

422. In elementary once more, your character finds themselves in a very unfortunate predicament. A bully has demanded that they be met after school in order for your character to, "get what's coming to them." Does your character meet them?

423. If so, how might this fight turn out?

424. Boy, your character has really let themselves go. They want to get back into shape to feel better and to entice their new love interest. How do they go about it?

425. Your character has just gotten into a fight with a sibling over something trivial. Further, it's entirely their fault. Does your character apologize first or wait on the other party to do so?

426. If they choose the former, what might their apology be like?

427. While travelling down a dark and ominous road your character comes across a bridge with light on the other side, clearly from a nearby township. There, your character is certain they will find food and relaxation. Before they can get there however, a large troll blocks their path demanding the answer to a riddle before granting entrance. How well do you suppose your character does at this riddle?

428. If your character does poorly, how might they decide to get across instead?

429. After a night drinking your character has a big hangover the next morning. How many drinks did it take to give them this result the previous night?

430. What was their night out like?

431. Your character is an accomplished scientist and has perfected genetics to the point where they can bring back one extinct animal. What animal would that be?

432. Suppose their experience in genetics also allows them to grant humanity one new gene. E.g. wings, a tail, or making everyone have perfect vision. What new evolutionary gift will they offer up to humanity?

433. Your character finds themselves trapped in quicksand while out exploring. There is no one around and if your character isn't careful, they

may find this their final resting place. How does your character try and save themselves?

434. Your character decides to write a song for the love of their life. What might the lyrics to this song be?

435. Your character visits an exotic pet store and finds that, not only is there every animal imaginable up for grabs, but that there is a special sale. Refusing to miss out on this once-in-a-lifetime opportunity your character decides to make a purchase. What kind of animal do they decide to buy?

436. Your character has decided to cook a romantic dinner for their date. Despite all of their efforts, it isn't long before black smoke billows from the oven. Dinner is burned! How does your character respond when the doorbell rings?

437. Your character has been set up on a blind date. When they arrive at the restaurant they see that the person they have been set up with is horribly unattractive. Does your character decide to get to know their date anyway?

438. Suppose your character's blind date is extremely attractive. Furthermore, they are successful and are very charming. When things seem too good to be true your character is hit with a bitter dose of reality as the blind date reveals that they engage in something illegal. How does your character respond?

439. Your character visits a local apothecary in order to buy a potion. What potion is it that they are buying?

440. During one trip to the zoo, a menacing tiger breaks free from their cage is headed straight towards you and a group of school children on their field trip. Does your character play the hero, make a run for it, or fall victim to the approaching predator?

441. Your character has suddenly been blessed with fire power. From their hands they can shoot fireballs and burn anything in their path. What is the first thing they do with this power?

442. While parked at a stop light, your character is suddenly rear-ended by a drunk driver. Before they have a chance to react, the other driver is already out of the car and screaming curses. What does your character do in response?

443. Your character has the flu. Yuck! After a sneezing, coughing, and fever fit all they want is to get a special home remedy. What might that remedy be?

444. After a wayward spell gone wrong (or perhaps right) your character is suddenly invisible for exactly 24 hours. How do they spend the day?

445. While on a road trip, your character's car breaks down in a strange city. What does your character decide to do?

446. While reading a book quietly in the park, an onlooker asks about your character's read. After

answering the first, second, and even the third time about the book's content the onlooker's questions don't seem to stop. What does your character do in response?

447. One day your character wakes up and finds out that they are permanently blind. What is the last visual they remember?

448. How will they cope to the sudden loss of sight?

449. After being in severe need of a haircut, your character visits their local salon. However, their usual stylist is out of town and only a novice is available. After receiving their haircut your character finds themselves completely bald. On a scale of 1-10, with 1 being polite and 10 being livid how do they react to this undesired haircut?

450. Your character finds themselves in the land of Oz. What do they ask the wizard for?

451. Sadly, your character's mother has just passed. They have been asked to deliver the eulogy. What words do they speak at the funeral?

452. While on a cruise ship your character unwittingly drops one of their most valuable pieces of jewelry into the ocean. How this happened remains a mystery. Does your character try and get it back?

453. A fortune teller predicts your character's death from the exact moment and manner in which they will die. Will your character try and escape this fate or will they succumb to it naturally?

454. On the streets of a seedy city, your character sees their worst enemy being attacked by bandits. Does your character try and intervene despite their hatred for the victim?

455. A strange man dressed in all black approaches your character. They tell your character that only they have a special set of skills that will help in an upcoming alien invasion. Does your character believe this strange man?

456. No matter the choice, what set of skills might be the man in black be referring to?

457. Your character has been sold into slavery. Chained, beaten, and nearly broken your character finally has a way to escape, but it is very risky. Will they take it?

458. Your character has been drafted into a war that they vehemently oppose. Will they defend their country anyway or try and find a way out of it?

459. Your character wakes up one day to find they are trapped in the body of a four year old. Luckily, they still have their adult mind. What is the first thing your character does?

460. After a being sent out on a space exploration mission your character has finally come across intelligent beings. As an ambassador of Earth, your character has been tasked with making first contact. What is that your character says to these beings from another world?

461. While out walking their dog in the middle of the night your character hears strange rustling coming from the bushes. Do they go and investigate?

462. If they do, what do you think your character might find there?

463. Your character is faced with the *Judgement of Paris* dilemma. They are given the following choices: the ability to rule the world through wisdom, to be victorious in battle, or to be guaranteed the love of their life. Which offer does your character choose?

464. Your character has just discovered that they are nothing more than a part of your imagination, in book form. How do they react?

465. Your character finds themselves being carried off by a dragon as part of their hoard. Once the dragon lands and dumps them into a pile of treasure, how might your character make their escape?

466. While your character is walking home alone at night a mugger suddenly jumps out and holds them at gunpoint. How does your character respond?

467. While swimming your character finds themselves caught in thick bundle of algae. No matter how hard they struggle, they become even more tangled. Their unfortunate fate seems to be inevitable. What are their last thoughts before drowning?

468. While listening on their amateur radio, your character suddenly picks up on a strange voice whispering that they are trapped inside the house and need help. It's very obvious your character is speaking to a ghost. Does your character try to locate the source of the sound and help?

469. If so, suppose your character finds the body of a murder victim. How might they try to set this hapless soul spirit free?

470. On your character's 16th birthday they finally learn the family secret. They have a curse that causes them to turn into werewolf every full moon. How well does your character react to their new change?

471. Your character has just been named King/Queen. What is their first ruling over their new subjects?

472. After making a trade with a witch, your character has been given second sight. How do they use this new gift?

473. Your character comes across a magic pill that lets them see through the eyes of another human being. What human do they choose to look through?

474. After looking through the eyes of another, what might they see?

475. Your character suddenly finds themselves inside a living musical. How do they respond to their new melodic life?

476. Your character is a transient that stows away on a train in order to find more work elsewhere. Where is that they are going?

477. Will they find what they are looking for?

478. It is Halloween night. What does your character decide to dress up as?

479. While walking in a busy city your character sees the person in front of them drop a $100 bill. Does your character decide to return it to them or engage in an act of thievery?

480. Your character wakes up one morning to find themselves in bed with stranger. They have a massive headache and briefly remember drinking the night before. What might this stranger look like?

481. Suppose the stranger says they want to get married now. How does your character respond?

482. While spending a hot summer night with friends your character is dared to go skinny dipping. Do they accept the challenge?

483. What if the dare took place in the middle of the day within eyeshot of gathered strangers?

484. Your character is sent a chain letter email promising them good fortune if they pass it along. Do they forward it?

485. Waking up in the middle of the night, your character looks out their window to see a faint glow. Upon closer inspection they find that it is the whole town holding pitchforks, torches, and

screaming the words "Monster!" How does your character react to this unfortunate turn of events?

486. While attending a fancy dinner party the lights suddenly go out and one of the guests is dead. A little while later and the same thing happens, leaving another dead body in the flickering lights. Clearly, there is a murderer loose and most likely, it's one of the other guests! How does your character go about solving the mystery?

487. Your character decides to fill out an online dating profile. What are some of the personal attributes they choose to highlight?

488. What would your character's ideal match be?

489. Your character discovers that they can suddenly read minds. Whose mind do they read first?

490. What do they discover about that person?

491. Your character is given a pop quiz at school. How well do they do on it?

492. After returning from a long day at work your character finds that they have somehow managed to lock themselves outside. Chances are the keys are back at work which is an hour drive. Does your character go back and get their keys or is there another alternative for getting back inside?

493. Your character finds themselves face-to-face with an angry witch who has felt wronged by them. In punishment the witch is going to take away one of your character's senses. Which one will it be?

494. Your character is entered into a singing competition and must sing or forfeit one million dollars. What song do they choose to sing?

495. While at a party a very attractive man/woman keeps hitting on your character. The only problem is that your character has a husband/wife back at home. Do they remain faithful?

496. Your character is put on the stand to testify at a murder trial. Although, they know the guilt of the accused party, your character also knows that the defendant has friends in very scary places. Does your character decide to tell the truth or lie?

497. What do they do after the trial is over?

498. Reaching the end of a life well-lived, your character now lies on their deathbed surrounded by all of their loved ones. What might their final words be?

499. Perhaps instead, your character is surrounded by all of their enemies. What would their final words be then?

500. Regretfully, your character has finally taken their last breath. As it turns out, there is an afterlife after all. Where is it they end up?

NON-TRADITIONAL CHARACTERS

Traditionally, many fiction characters are heterosexual adult males and females. However, diversity itself should be lauded and as such, it is important to consider when that mold is broken. What if you decide to write for teens or young children? What if your character decides to forgo all constructs of gender for something more androgynous? Or, perhaps your character is an animal or an alien? Further still, what if your character hits on all three types? First and foremost, it is important to continue to consider the humanity in these characters; even if they are not human. A great example of this is when an interviewer once told George R.R. Martin, author of the *A Song of Ice and Fire* series, "I noticed that you write women really well and really different. Where does that come from?"

To which Martin replied, "You know, I've always considered women to be people."

In this vein, this section was added to help those who write non-traditional characters and want a fuller springboard to work with. However, it is important that one does not consider the addition of these sections as a crutch. These characters should be fully fleshed out and more often than not, treating these characters as you would the stereotypical, traditional characters makes them far more authentic than simply treating them as an "other". With that in mind, use these questions to build richer backstories, personalities, and appearances rather than concentrating on that perceived otherness.

Young Characters

Young characters can be especially hard to write because, more often than not, our adult minds have already experienced a vast amount of situations that most kids haven't even dreamed of. Even the most mundane tasks, such as paying taxes or the aches and pain that comes with aging, are beyond the scope of a child's mind. As such, characterization, especially for young characters, can completely make or break a plotline. Whether your young characters are in the background or front and center, each character must be believable, which means you need to understand how a child thinks and acts.

501. Does your character act much older than they are biologically?
502. What about younger?
503. Are they considered a "cute" kid or traditionally attractive if they are a teenager?
504. In what way?
505. Are they considered traditionally ugly, whether as a child or teen?
506. In what way?
507. Does your character feel like they need to eschew the role that has been mapped out for them? I.e. Their parents or guardians want them to be a knight, but they would rather be a baker.
508. What do they want to be when they grow up?

509. Will there be a lot in the way of achieving that goal? I.e. The character comes from a poor background, but one day they want to be very wealthy.

510. Are they more concerned with responsibilities or having fun?

511. When taking on responsibilities, whether minor or major, are they prone to complaining or are they proud to achieve certain goals?

512. Do they have responsibilities that most children their age do not?

513. What is it?

514. Who placed this responsibility on them?

515. Do they have any animosity towards that person or group?

516. Do they have to take care of someone other than themselves? E.g. the family pet, young brothers and sisters, etc.

517. When having fun, do they enjoy spending most of their free time alone or with a group?

518. If with a group, who do they spend most of their time with?

519. If alone, what do they enjoy doing?

520. Are they treated strangely because of it?

521. Does your character have a best friend?

522. Who is it?

523. Does your character have a crush?

524. Who is it?

525. Would they ever act on this crush? I.e. ask someone they like out.

526. Does your character have a world view they have built for themselves or based around what they have been taught?

527. What is it?

528. If this view is based on what they have been taught, who taught them?

529. If it is based on something they have gathered themselves, how did they come about it?

530. On that note, is your character aware of the darkness of the world? E.g. they know that everything must die, they know that bad things sometimes happen to good people, etc.

531. If so, do they feel like there is something they can do to change the world or do they feel that they will just have to accept life as it is?

532. If they feel like they can one day change the world, are they taking an active role now or are they waiting until adulthood?

533. In what ways have they accepted the negativity of the world?

534. What does the character think about themselves? E.g. their appearance, their personality, etc.

535. Are they actively trying to change certain aspects of themselves?

536. If so, is this because of a negative aspect they have found or based on what others have told them?

537. If it is the latter, who pointed out this flaw?

538. Does your character keep any kind of traditional memento for a child that age? E.g. yearbook, journal, diary, photo albums, etc.

539. What might be contained within its pages? E.g. the journal might have their day-to-day activities, their yearbook may only have signatures from close friends, etc.

540. Do they keep anything else from their childhood? E.g. collecting ticket stubs, Valentine cards, etc.

541. Have they ever tried to run away?

542. If so, was it for adventure, desire to rebel, or because of a bad home life?

543. If the home life was bad, who caused the negativity?

544. Does your character feel like they have a lot of input into their day-to-day life or is everything decided for them?

545. Do they rebel often?

546. What they normally do when rebelling against authority?

547. Whose authority do they typically rebel against? E.g. their parents or guardians, the law, the highest fraction of the land, etc.

548. Do they find it hard to rebel or very, very easy? I.e. they always second guess themselves thinking they will "get in trouble."

549. On that note, is the character a traditional goody-two-shoes or a "bad kid?"

550. As an infant, did your character cry often?

551. As an infant, did they complete "firsts" faster than their peers? E.g. stood on their own first, talked in full sentences by three, etc.

552. As an infant, was your character held often or coddled in anyway?

553. By who?

554. In the toddler stage, were they considered bratty?

555. In what way?

556. In childhood, were they prone to getting "sick" in order to avoid certain school activities? I.e. telling their parent they are too sick to go to school in order to avoid picture day.

557. Do they have trouble paying attention in class or are they more likely to get the concepts before the other children?

558. Are they highly communicative, able to voice their needs or concerns, or they keep everything bottled up inside?

559. Would they be considered a teacher's pet?

560. What about a class clown?

561. At what age did they first realize their body was changing?

562. Was this a particularly awkward time for them?

563. In what way?

564. On graduation day would they be more likely to be the Valedictorian or be last in their class?

565. If they would be a Valedictorian, what would their speech be?

566. Would you say your character will change significantly as they get older, or will they be true to the same personality they had when they were younger?

567. Does your character have friends and comrades that will be there for their rest of their life? (Death and other obstacles notwithstanding).

568. What about family members?

569. What kind of obstacles does your character currently face?

570. How are they handling them?

571. Do they have a strong support system to help overcome these problems?

572. Who is within that support system?

573. Do they enjoy having this support system or do they feel like they must handle their own problems?

574. Do they often feel they must take on life's challenges by themselves?

575. Does your character have a specific destiny that will affect them at a certain age? E.g. they are the chosen one, they will become king, etc.

576. What's the age?

577. What is the destiny?

Now for some scenarios geared specifically towards young characters:

578. While out playing with a group of friends an old abandoned house is found. One of the friends

dares your character to enter it and take any valuables found. Does your character do it?

579. What if the house was supposedly haunted?

580. While exploring their parent's closet one day your character stumbles across an old photo album. Inside they find evidence of an older brother or sister that they never knew about. Do they inquire about the strange occurrence or investigate on their own?

581. While walking home from school your character finds an orphaned puppy. They've always wanted a pet, but their parents or guardians have made it clear that no pets are allowed. Do they find some way to smuggle the canine home?

582. If they are set on keeping the pup, how do they go about doing it?

583. There is a new kid in school that seems very "weird" in traditional standards. Unsurprisingly, the other kids began to tease and make fun of them. Does your character join in or stand up for them?

584. If your character has decided to tease them, what kind of insults might they say?

585. If your character is going to stand up to them, how might they go about doing it? Especially because they seem to be the only one not joining in on the teasing.

586. Your character is next in line to be King or Queen. However, they catch wind that a younger

sibling plans to kill them so that they can take the throne. How does your character react?

587. Your character's room is a complete mess! Angrily, their parents or guardians tell them if they do not clean it, they will lose half the toys in the room. Does your character get to cleaning, try to negotiate, or outright refuse?

588. Your character is allowed to invite a friend over for a visit. It is the very first time the friend has come over and your character is excited. What is the first thing in the room your character shows their friend?

589. It's the first day of at a new school and your character has inadvertently managed to embarrass themselves. By afternoon they are ready to crawl into a dark hole. When their parents or guardians ask them how their day was do they lie or tell them the truth?

590. What might this horrible, no good, very bad day be like?

591. While eavesdropping in the teacher's lounge, your character hears a horrible secret about everyone's favorite educator. Do they tell everyone the big secret or keep it under wraps?

592. If your character decides to divulge the secret, who might they tell?

593. Unfortunately, your character has come down with the chicken pox! How might they pass the time to keep from scratching?

594. Your character begins to volunteer at a local animal shelter. Very quickly, they learn that animals that do not get adopted are, unfortunately, euthanized. How might they react to this horrible news?

595. Perhaps at that same shelter the animals are being mistreated. When one of the attendants goes off on break there is a chance to free all of the animals. Does your character seize the moment?

596. Your character and a group of friends discover an old cave while hiking. Once there they find a skeleton! How does your character respond?

597. While drawing in a notebook one day your character suddenly finds that whatever they draw will come to life. What is it that they draw next?

598. Every night before bed your character is read to before they fall asleep. They are always given a choice of what story it will be. What book do they reach for each time?

599. While exploring outside your character comes across an injured bird. What might they do to help the poor creature?

600. Your character suddenly finds themselves in an orphanage after being abandoned. How might they deal with the new change?

601. On the opposite end of the spectrum, your character's family suddenly becomes very, very wealthy. Does your character lose sight of where they have come from?

602. After a horrible car crash, your character finds that the other occupants are not moving. Do they go for help, stay put, or panic?

603. Your character starts to hang out with a group of kids who begin to dwell in increasingly bad behavior. First it is stealing candy from stores, then bullying, and finally, it escalates with the desire to take a human life. Will your character continue to join the fray?

604. Your character has gotten detention! What was the infraction?

605. In detention they are allowed to spend their time working on school work or writing. What do they do specifically?

606. Your character develops their first crush, but before they can act on it, their crush begins to date someone else. Your character knows this is a very bad kid. Do they warn their intended or simply let it play out?

607. Your character finds themselves trapped in the woods with the sound of wolves all around. Are they resourceful enough to survive or will the grownups take on the search for their body in the morning?

608. If they choose to be resourceful, how might they survive their night in the woods?

609. Your character decides to enter the school's science fair. What project will they enter?

610. Your character's family has another child. How does your character cope?

611. Perhaps this child slowly begins to receive most of the attention, how might the character cope then?

612. Your character has been tasked with babysitting for the first time. Eagerly, they begin to make an itinerary for what kind of activities they might use with the younger children. What might this itinerary include?

613. At school, the lunchroom suddenly erupts into a food fight. What part has your character played in this silly event? E.g. they are the one that started the food fight, it took them by surprise, etc.

614. Your character stumbles across a website that they should not be looking at. Suddenly their parent walks in before they have a chance to change browsers. How does your character respond?

615. Your character must collect a great deal of money in order to participate in a club event. How might they go about doing it? E.g. bake sale, car wash, etc.

616. One day your character seriously begins to doubt the current moral code (whether religious-based or simply the family creed) of their parents or guardians. Do they go against the grain without telling them, explain how they feel, or continue to pretend the belief is shared?

617. It's Thanksgiving Day and your character has been waiting for hours for the meal to be ready. When their parent's back is turned they see some of the pies in plain view. Does your character give in to temptation?

618. It's the night of the school play and your character is a nervous wreck. How might they deal with their uncontrollable butterflies?

619. Your character suddenly finds themselves in a tale similar to *Hansel and Gretel*. How might they best the evil witch?

620. After asking their parents or guardians all day your character is finally given permission to go swimming. Just as they enter the pool, a roll of thunder can be heard in the distance and soon, rain begins to pour down heavily. Does your character swim anyway despite the risks?

621. Your character has been given a new pet and are tasked with taking care of it – from cleaning up its messes to feeding and grooming the creature. Does the novelty wear off or does the character accept the responsibilities wholeheartedly?

622. While swimming at the lake your character suddenly hears a scream from somewhere in the middle of the water. A friend is in the middle of drowning! How does your character respond?

623. Your character has a horrible nightmare that they can't seem to shake. At first, their parents or guardians are sympathetic, but after weeks they simply reply that it's time for the character to face

things on their own. How does your character react to the mere thought?

624. Your character finds themselves in a fight at school with a known bully. Would they be the loser or the one to come out on top?

625. Whether or not they lose, would your character try to keep this fact from their parents or guardians?

626. After inviting a friend over, the friend inadvertently breaks a very special possession that belongs to your character. How do they respond?

627. What if the object belonged to another member of the house?

628. Your character goes to a new school and begins to be teased mercilessly. What might the teasing include?

629. How might your character respond to the slights against them?

630. Unfortunately, your character realizes that they are short three credits from graduation. They can easily get the credits in a summer class and graduate with their class, but it's in a course they hate. Do they take it anyway?

631. What might the course be?

632. Your character finds themselves led astray by an old witch. Too late they find out their action has led to their own doom. However, they can try to fight back and save other children from the same fate. Are they brave enough?

633. Your character suddenly finds themselves in a world without adults. How do they react to the strange change?

634. While stargazing one night your character sees a strange object fall to the ground through a dazzling blaze. Wherever the object has landed seems to be in walking distance. Do they go and investigate?

635. Your character has a paper due tomorrow night! They know it is their own fault for procrastinating, but if they don't turn something in they'll fail the entire course. Do they buckle down and come up with an A-worthy paper, wing it, or simply give up?

636. Your character wakes up to find that they have wet the bed. It's not only embarrassing, but your character also finds that they do not feel good either. It's in the middle of the night so no one else in the house will be up for hours. Does your character take matters into their own hands by cleaning the mess or do they wake up another occupant?

637. If they wake someone else up, who do they turn to in this time of need?

638. Your character receives a strange text message from someone they do not know. At first they choose to ignore the threatening message, but then the unknown number mentions personal information. How does your character respond?

639. Your character finds an object that will turn them into a grownup instantly. Do they choose to use this strange object?

640. If they choose to use the object, what age might they choose to grow up to?

641. As a grownup, what is the first thing they do?

642. Your character is about to take their very first ride on a dragon. What kind of emotions might they be feeling?

643. It's the night before the first day of school and your character must pack their book bag. What items might they put inside?

644. Your character stumbles across an old and ancient creature trapped inside a cage. The creature begs to be let out, but your character has heard warnings about trusting strangers, especially strange creatures. Do they let it out anyway?

645. While walking home from school your character suddenly sees a neighbor's house catch on fire. The occupants inside begin screaming. There doesn't seem to be anyone around for miles. How does your character respond?

646. While walking through the woods one day your character meets an old wise man who offers them one bit of advice that will shape their future forever. What might this advice be?

647. Does your character take this piece of wisdom?

648. Your character is told that if they finish all their chores by the end of the day then they can have

all their friends come over. Unfortunately, when the deadline rolls around your character is still not finished. How do they deal with their disappointment?

649. Your character is given a chance to start life over with a brand new family. Do they decide to accept?

650. Why/Why not?

651. Your character stumbles across a vicious wolf that wants to gobble them up whole. The wolf doesn't seem very smart, but he is very powerful. How does your character get out of the situation?

652. Your character goes on a game show with their family for a chance to win a huge prize. By the end of the competition it's all up to your character for the win. How do they handle the pressure?

653. Suppose the character and their family do win, but the prize is a trip for a certain amount of individuals. One of the family members has to sit out. Does your character give up this once in a lifetime opportunity or do they demand someone else do so?

654. Your character has decided to bake some delicious treats to take to their grandmother's house. What might they pack for her?

655. While walking home from school your character sees a strange dark van following them. At first, they think it might be in their head, but when the car has trailed them for two blocks straight, they

become less sure. How do to they deal with the stranger?

656. Your character has decided they want to start their own collection. What is it they will start collecting?

657. When your character comes home from school they are met with furious parents or guardians. Very simply, your character is simply told, "I know what you did." What is it they have done?

658. Your character is told that there are not enough soldiers for an invading army and the character is now old enough to fight. Does your character welcome the chance to fight for their land or are they very afraid?

659. If it is the latter, would your character choose to shirk their responsibility by turning coward and running away?

660. Your character catches their best friend stealing from the store. Although the friend doesn't get caught, the item they have taken is very valuable. Does your character confront them, tell the shop keep, or do nothing at all?

661. Your character stumbles across a wounded animal that will not make it. Does your character choose to put the poor creature out of its misery?

662. Your character receives their very own bike after years borrowing from their older sibling. Where do they decide to go to first?

663. What if they receive their own car?

664. While out riding a horse your character is suddenly thrown off. Not only are they startled but it seems they have also broken a leg. There is no one around for miles. What does your character do?

665. Your character has heard the old idiom, "Never talk to strangers" on more than one occasion. However, when they stumble across a poor soul in need of help do they lend a hand or do they move on?

666. While rummaging through an old attic your character finds a box that contains a servant of the dark. This evil creature can be commanded, but bad consequences will arise. Does your character give the minion a command anyway?

667. Your character has done something wrong, but is allowed to pick their own punishment. Do they choose timeout, corporal punishment, or to have something taken away?

668. Your character realizes that adulthood is not that far away. In fact, they have a summer left before they will hit that big milestone. What do they spend their summer doing?

LGBT+ Characters

As many would agree, the spectrum of sexuality is an extremely complex one. In fact, the term LGBT, which stands for lesbian, gay, bisexual, and transgender is often in itself sometimes seen as exclusive of certain sexuality types. For this purpose, one might find the term LGBTQ (lesbian, gay bisexual, transgender,

and queer) to be more appropriate as well as the LGBTQIA
acronym (which adds "intersex" and "asexual) to be formidable.
No matter what acronym one uses it is important to keep in mind,
once again, that these characters should not be written in a way that
dictates otherness. To illustrate the point, one might run into the
same wall when the individual is a male writing a female character,
an able bodied character writing a disabled character, or when
writing a character in an entirely different race. The point is not to
create a stereotype or build a character that seems overtly sexualized
or written as a joke, but rather one should use these questions as a
platform to fully understand who these characters are as a person.
No matter how they view themselves.

669. What sexual orientation does your character identify as? E.g. gay, bisexual, pansexual, etc.
670. What sexual orientation are they perceived by others? I.e. the character is gay, but everyone believes they are heterosexual.
671. Is this by choice?
672. If not how is that choice been hindered?
673. If this is because of a person, who is that person?
674. If they choose to identify outside of the realm of sexuality, such as being androgynous, in what way do they make this known? E.g. informing others, choosing to wear both male and female clothes, etc.
675. Are they more effeminate, masculine, or a little bit of both?
676. In what ways do they express this?

677. At what age did they realize they were not traditionally heterosexual?

678. How did they cope with this knowledge?

679. Did they tell anyone?

680. If so, how did that person(s) react?

681. Aside from their reaction, did your character find a lot of support with disclosing their sexual orientation?

682. If support was granted, in what way?

683. If no support was found, how did your character cope?

684. Has your character been intimate with members of their preferred gender?

685. At what age was their first encounter?

686. In terms of awkward versus very sensual and exciting, how was that experience for them?

687. Did this initial relationship last?

688. In terms of relationships as a whole, have they been largely positive or negative?

689. If positive, why have these relationships ended?

690. If largely negative, what has been the biggest barrier?

691. What has been the longest lasting relationship?

692. Why did this particular relationship end?

693. Does your character have a strong support system currently?

694. If so, who is included?

695. Does your character use any kind of coping mechanisms against any bigotry they find? E.g.

they attend LGBT+ meetings, they drink or take drugs, etc.

696. Are these coping mechanisms healthy or harmful?
697. Do any members of their support system know of these coping mechanisms?
698. Has your character been exposed to any type of prejudices?
699. What were the incidents?
700. Was the culprit a single person or a group?
701. Who was the person?
702. If it was a group, what group was it?
703. Did any of the situations involve violence?
704. Was a member(s) of authority called? E.g. law enforcement, school principal, parents, etc.
705. Did the other party get arrested or did those in authority turn a blind eye?
706. How did your character handle these situations?
707. If any kind of revenge was extracted, how did your character go about seeking it?
708. Did your character themselves get in trouble with law enforcement or another person of authority as a result?
709. In general, does your character find that many members of authority turn a blind eye?
710. In what way?
711. In general, does your character find that the general community where they live is not accepting?
712. In what way?

713. Has your character ever moved or changed locations because of this?
714. Where did they originally hail from?
715. Where did they go as a result?
716. Was their individual situation better or worse when they got their?
717. Does your character feel like they should change this fundamental aspect of themselves?
718. In what way?
719. If given a choice, would your character change their sexuality or are they proud to be who they are?
720. Contrary to how they feel now, has this perception changed over time?
721. In what way?
722. Does your character's sexuality go against their religion, moral code, or their own perceived ethics?
723. In what way?
724. If so, how have they dealt with this perception?
725. Do others know of this perception?
726. Who?
727. How do family members view this self-discrimination?
728. Friends?
729. Lovers?
730. Politically, what kind of viewpoints does your character have on their sexuality?
731. Does their support system share these political viewpoints?

732. If given the chance, would your character support or oppose gay marriage?
733. What about polyamorous unions?
734. What about other types of unions?
735. What are they?
736. Does your character desire to eventually be married?
737. What would their ideal marriage be like?
738. If they do not want to be married, do they eschew the idea of marriage altogether?
739. Why?
740. Does your character eschew long-lasting relationships in general?
741. Why?
742. Does your character imagine themselves having children one day?
743. Why/Why not?
744. Will their partner bear the responsibility of child rearing (and/or birthing if applicable) or will that duty be taken on by your character?
745. What would your character's ideal partner be like?
746. When your character thinks of the word "family", what is the ideal scenario to them?
747. Do they believe they will one day achieve that goal?
748. Why/Why not?
749. Going back to politics once again, is your character involved heavily in politics?
750. In what way?

751. Does your character attend demonstrations, rallies, or other shows of support?
752. Envisioning a protest or support sign the character might hold, what would it say?
753. Within a protest what might your character's demonstration style be like? E.g. angry yelling, silence, passiveness, etc.
754. If a member of the other side turned violent, how would your character react?
755. If a member of the other side needed help would your character lend a hand?
756. If so, would they have a limit to their charity?
757. If not, what would their reaction be then?
758. Aside from any type of political demonstrations, is your character heavily involved with members of the same sexuality group?
759. In what way?
760. Does your character feel like their sexuality limits their life goals?
761. In what way?
762. Has your character lost out to someone else because of their sexuality? E.g. they would be heir to a throne but cannot, they lost out of a job promotion, etc.
763. What was the reaction of the other party?
764. Of your character?
765. Does your character feel like this will change in the foreseeable future?

766. How does your character feel like the world will change (towards their sexuality group) in five years?

767. In ten years?

768. In twenty years?

Now for some scenarios geared specifically towards LGBT+ characters:

769. In middle school your character has their very first crush, only it's not who they intended it to be. How do they deal with this new awakening?

770. After years of living with their partner, your character is finally ready to settle down and raise a child. Only their partner isn't. How does your character approach the subject once more?

771. What if the roles were versed and your character did not want a child, but their partner continued to bring up the subject?

772. Quite unexpectedly your character has fallen in love with their best friend. The biggest problem is that this friend is already in a committed relationship. Does your character bring up the subject or try to push it back down?

773. Your character has decided it is time for a new look to celebrate who they really are inside. What might this new style look like?

774. A powerful and cruel witch decides to curse your character and their partner, turning your character

into the opposite gender. Not only are they this new gender, but they do not even look the same. How does your character go about getting their partner to fall in love with them again?

775. Suppose that your character *is* the witch or warlock, and are doing this to a heterosexual couple. What might their goal be?

776. While attending a rally your character meets someone they fall in love with on first sight. During the course of the evening the two share a kiss before parting ways. Your character is desperate to find this person again. How do they go about doing searching for their missed connection?

777. While in class your character's professor begins to give a lecture that is very anti-lgbt+. Does your character stand up for themselves or remain under the radar?

778. The end of the world has occurred and the human race is almost wiped out. *Almost* being the operative word. It seems the only person left, aside from your character, is someone that they loathe. How might they cope?

779. Your character begins to have a strange reoccurring dream that causes them to question everything they know about themselves. Do they try to make the dreams stop or do they explore these feelings further?

780. In order to cope with society's lack of acceptance your character starts to give into some undesirable temptations. What might that be?

781. How do they get out of it?

782. Your character has finally decided to live life as who they were meant to be. Several years later they meet an old classmate who treated them extremely harshly when they were younger. How does your character react?

783. What if this old classmate had finally embraced their hidden sexuality as well?

784. Your character has finally decided to let their friends and family know about their once-hidden sexuality. How do they go about it?

785. Suppose your character has decided to pen a letter to a crush. What might this letter include?

786. While they were younger your character overhears their parents or guardians having a serious discussion about the character. Years later, this discussion still bubbles to their memory. What might this discussion have been about?

787. Does your character eventually confront their parents or guardians about the discussion?

788. Your character's best friend dies and rather than letting their children go through the adoption system, your character has decided to take them in. How does your character cope with the new responsibility?

789. Your character is kidnapped off the street one day. Unsure of what they have done they slowly realize that they have been taken by a religious movement that wants to set a horrible example. How does your character manage to escape?

790. A career-obsessed character suddenly loses their job when their hidden sexuality is found out. They can deny the claim, fight back, or start to look for another job. What do they choose to do?

791. If they deny the claim, how might they refute the evidence?

792. If they choose to fight back, how do they go about doing so?

793. If they look for a job, where would they look first?

794. Your character has decided to start an LGBT+ club on campus. The only problem is, they must figure out how to get new recruits. How might they go about doing so?

795. What kind of activities might your character plan for initiation?

796. Your character has been tasked with giving a presentation in class, as a representative of the sexuality the class is studying. How does your character prepare?

797. What might this lecture entail?

798. During the middle of the night your character awakens to the sound of breaking glass. Quickly, they run to the kitchen where the noise was heard. Unfortunately, once there they discover that a

brick has been through the window with an ugly note attached. What might this note say?

799. How does your character deal with the transgression against them?

800. It's a historic day for the LGBT+ community, but for very terrible reasons. A new law would have them rounded up and held under a new law. Your character has become something of a rebel leader, fighting against this injustice. What is the first plan of action they take?

801. Your character has decided to craft a mix tape for their family and friends as a way of "coming out." What tracks might be included?

802. It has been 100 years since new marriage laws have been overturned. Times are very peaceful for all sexualities and walks of life. Then one day there is a murmuring of a rogue group that wants to send everything back into the dark ages. Your character catches wind that a friend is involved. How do they confront the former ally?

803. Your character goes through a photo album of what they used to look like before they decided to become who they were always meant to be. What kind of thoughts go through their mind?

804. After several years of marriage your character must finally come to grips with the fact that this is not the individual, or the gender, they want to spend forever with. They respect their partner

and thus, want to let them down in the easiest way possible. How might they go about it?

805.   In the same scenario, how would your character respond if the reaction was solely negative?

806.   While living their life happily, an old enemy shows up with a few photographs showing what your character used to look like when they were younger, and before they decided to become who they were meant to be. How does your character deal with this blast from the past?

807.   Your character discovers a time machine and can go back to a past point in their own life. They choose to have a heart-to-heart with their younger self. What might they say?

808.   Suppose your character's younger self refuses to believe a word of what is said. How might your character get through to them then?

809.   Your character has been hired as a new teacher at a very affluent school. However, when their sexuality is found out your character is quickly fired. How does your character fight back against this act of discrimination?

810.   Your character decides to write a memoir about their struggles in life. What might the title be?

811.   What kind of content might the story contain?

812.   Imagine that the story becomes an instant bestseller and your character is suddenly thrust into a life of luxury. The problem is that there is a huge amount of pressure, especially from those

looking up to your character. How might they cope?

813. When they were younger your character is told a bit of wisdom that absolutely saves them later down the line, when life is incredibly harsh. What was this sage piece of advice?

814. Who was it that gave them this bit of wisdom?

815. After a really bad breakup, your character's partner has moved out, seemingly taking all of their things with them. As it turns out, there is one item left and it holds a great deal of sentimentality. What might that item be?

816. What was it that caused the breakup in the first place?

817. One day your character is sent an anonymous box. Inside it is supposed to contain something that will help them get through an especially trying time. What might be contained inside?

818. Who might have sent it?

819. Your character hears on the radio that several LGBT+ individuals have been hurt by way of a hate crime and are now recuperating in the hospital. Although your character does not know these individuals, they decide to help out anyway. In what way do they lend a hand?

820. Your character has decided to invent a brand new word that better reflects their sexuality. What might that new word be?

821. To fight against injustice your character decides to create an organization that will better help individuals in the LGBT+ community. What might the motto for this organization be?

822. With a sparkling political career your character is suddenly blackmailed with images taken of them and a lover. Do they decide to proceed with their campaign knowing that these images will most likely be released anyway?

823. Your character suddenly finds themselves strapped to a chair in a very dark room. Very soon an individual in white scrubs comes by and announces that the conversion therapy will begin soon. How does your character manage to escape the horrifying situation?

824. In the middle of the night your character receives a phone call regarding their closest friend. It seems they have been assaulted while walking home because of their orientation. How does your character respond?

825. Does your character choose to seek retaliation?

826. In what way?

827. Your character receives the horrifying news that a family member has passed. Unfortunately, this person always treated them poorly because of their orientation. How does your character take the news that they're gone?

828. The marriage laws have been updated to reflect changing viewpoints. What might your character's ideal wedding look like?

829. Your character and their partner have opted to adopt a child from another country. However, on the big day the adoption falls through. Your character, their partner, and even the child are already sold on this new family unit. How does your character respond?

830. Suppose the problem was not some form of technical or legal error, but rather outright discrimination. How does your character respond then?

831. Suppose the adoption goes through, but when the child arrives home they are the complete opposite of how they appeared in their home location. This can be due to appearance, personality, and so forth. Does your character accept them with open arms anyway?

832. If your character responds positively, and makes the best of the situation, suppose their partner has the opposite reaction. Your character's partner wants to send the child back. Does your character give in?

833. Your character is on a date with someone they have liked for a long time. Just as dinner gets underway the couple next to them begin to sling inappropriate slurs at your character and their partner. How does your character react to this slight?

834. During a road trip your character has a tire blow out in the middle of a very conservative town.

The only alternative, besides simply waiting for someone to pass by, is to walk to a nearby gas station, but there is no telling what the people might be like once your character arrives. Do they wait for help or choose to go anyway?

835.   After a lifetime of living in shame and being burdened by opposing viewpoints, your character is finally able to settle down with the one they love. Unfortunately, it is at an extremely old age. How might they choose to celebrate?

Nonhuman Characters

For many writers, nonhuman characters are some of the most difficult to write, whether aliens or animals. This is often because, like with young characters, we are only seeing the world with our adult human mind. The world for these creatures is extremely nuanced and complex. For example, suppose your animal character only communicates through the use of pheromones? What if your extreme human, such as a fairy or a vampire, hasn't been amongst humans for thousands of years? In all of these cases you must find a way to draw out the uniqueness of the species while still allowing the reader to relate in some way. The best way to do that is to use these questions in order to fully understand the biological and social needs of your species, while still allowing that extremely important human connection.

836.   Is your character bipedal or does it stand upright?

837.   Does it have fur, feathers, or something else entirely?

838. What about additional appendages such as a tail, horns, or extra limbs?

839. Does your character have a unique appearance from others of is species?

840. In what way?

841. Does it have a specific coat pattern or other markings that separate it from other members of its species, or is a reflection of the species in general?

842. How so?

843. How does your character communicate with members of its species?

844. With others outside of its species?

845. Does this communication pattern change if the character is injured?

846. What about excited?

847. Threatened?

848. Does your character have any other mode of communication? E.g. body language, releasing certain smells, telepathy, etc.

849. Does your character have an extremely keen sense of smell?

850. Does your character have very strong hearing?

851. Does your character have excellent or above average eyesight?

852. Are these extraordinary senses unique to the species?

853. Did your character come from Earth or somewhere else entirely?

854. What is their primary habitat like?

855. What happens if they step outside of that habitat?

856. Are they highly adaptable to their surroundings?

857. No matter if they are adaptable or not, does your character get homesick easily?

858. Do they have unique needs that they can only get from their primary habitat? I.e. their only food source is plants grown there.

859. What kind of foods do they eat?

860. Would they be considered more predator or prey?

861. Do they feed off of humans?

862. In general, how do they feel towards humans?

863. Are humans aware of their existence?

864. If applicable, would a human make a good companion for friendship?

865. What about a romantic interest?

866. If applicable, would it be possible to mate with a human?

867. What about becoming allies?

868. On a social level, or they considered above or below humans?

869. How does your character personally feel towards humans?

870. Is there another species that they are very adverse to?

871. In what way?

872. How does your character personally feel towards that particular species?

873. Are there any types of hybrids of your character's species?

874. What might these hybrid types look like?
875. What about different types or races of the species in general? I.e. one type has certain markings while others do not.
876. What type/race does your character belong to?
877. Are these races/types against each other in terms of conflict?
878. In what way?
879. How does your character personally feel about these other types/races?
880. Amongst their species, what rank does your character hold? E.g. alpha, beta, etc.
881. Is your character happy being in this position?
882. How is this position generally earned? I.e. they had to have fought with another member of the tribe.
883. How is the highest position generally earned?
884. What roles and responsibilities does this position require?
885. How does the species as a whole treat members of this ranking?
886. What about the highest ranking?
887. The lowest?
888. In general, does the species work as a tribe, pack, or some other type of unit?
889. Are there several branches to this tribe, pack, unit, etc.?
890. Which one does your character belong to?

891. Are they loyal to this group, or does their loyalty lay elsewhere?

892. Does the species have strong familial ties?

893. In what way?

894. Are these inner species groups at odds with each other?

895. In what way?

896. Does your species hunt collectively or individually?

897. Does your character prefer being around members of its own kind or alone?

898. Is your character considered an integral part of the tribe?

899. Is your character curious about humans?

900. What about other species?

901. Does your character have a good relationship with humans?

902. Around humans would your character be fearful or more mistrusting?

903. Does your character's species have any particular rituals or ceremonies that are observed?

904. Does your character observe these important dates?

905. How close does the species feel to nature?

906. What about the manmade world?

907. Does your character's species feel like it has a duty to protect something? E.g. of nature, of an ancient power, etc.

908. Does your character shirk this responsibility?

909. In what way?

910. Does the species have any mating rituals?
911. What about breeding or courtship rituals?
912. Does the species mate for life?
913. Does your character currently have a life mate?
914. Who is it?
915. How many offspring does the species typically have?
916. Are offspring generally reared until adulthood or is there a breaking away from the original family unit much earlier?
917. Does your character keep particular customs of is species?
918. Would your character be likely to share these customs with anyone? I.e. a human ally.
919. Is love a concept within the species?
920. Would your character consider loving a human?
921. Is your character considered a warrior type?
922. Is your character more passive and nonaggressive?
923. Does your character themselves feel at one with nature?
924. What about the world of mankind?
925. Is your character a good hunter?
926. Good gatherer?
927. Has your character ever killed a member of its species?
928. Another species?
929. A human?
930. Is there any kind of specific ritual in death?
931. In birth/life?

932. How long is the life cycle of the species?

933. Is the species' life cycle very different from a human's? E.g. they do not have a puberty stage, they have an additional stage, they do not age, etc.

934. Does the species have their own moral code, different from that of a human's?

935. What is it?

Now for some scenarios geared specifically towards nonhuman characters:

936. While deep in the forest your character comes across a wounded animal. It has been a long time since your character has had a meal, but there's no telling if this animal is diseased or not. Does your character take a bite anyway?

937. Your character's role as a leader is threatened when an underling decides to revolt. How does your character deal with the transgression?

938. Your character has come across a human for the very first time. First, your character responds with mild curiosity...then they realize that humans can be very, very dangerous. How does your character deal with this new enemy?

939. Your character is in a very compromising situation and must rely solely on its instincts; especially that which separates it from other types of creatures. What might these special animal instincts be?

940. How does your character use them to their fullest?

941. Your character has decided that it wants to become human. The only way to do this is to turn its back on its family and live amongst man. How does your character break it to their tribe?

942. After getting into a fight your character is severely wounded. It is not fatal, but it will become so if they do not get medical attention right away. The only problem is that they are in the middle of nowhere. How do they manage to save themselves?

943. In your character's culture it is common practice to be mated for life. Once a life mate is chosen they will then settle down and have offspring. The problem arises when their mate cannot bear children. How does your character cope?

944. What if it was your character that could not bear offspring?

945. After waking up one morning your character does not recognize any of their surroundings. Fear instantly sets in when they realize they are in a strange enclosure, set upon them by a mad scientist who wants to learn more about the species. How does your character escape?

946. In a similar scenario, suppose your character has been caught in a trap by a determined hunter. If your character does not act quickly their head just might become a mount on the wall. What does your character do?

947. After overthrowing the former leader your character must now establish a brand new social order within its tribe. What might this new hierarchy be like?

948. A group of nefarious humans have rounded up your character and a number of its species. Soon your character finds themselves trapped inside a large dome with others of its kind. Around the dome humans cheer. The rules are simple; the last one left alive is the winner. Does your character intend to be the last one standing, or will they try to find some way for everyone to make it out alive?

949. Suppose your character is forced to fight members of a different species, or many different species. How might things change then?

950. Your character has tasted human flesh for the very first time. How did this strange occurrence come about?

951. Suppose your character was forced to against their will. How might your character respond to the transgression?

952. Your character has managed to eat food that turned their stomach after the first few mouthfuls. That's because it's poisonous! Does your character give into their fate or try to save their own hide in some way?

953. In a similar scenario imagine that there is simply nothing they can do. How does your character cope with the inevitable?

954. While out meandering in the snowy woods your character finds themselves caught by a rusted bear trap. How do they manage to escape?

955. Your character wakes up to the sounds of chanting outside of its home. Upon inspection they soon learn that an animal rights group has taken up your character's species as their newest cause. Does your character enjoy this new development or are they annoyed with all the ruckus?

956. Your character is in a power struggle with another member of the group. There has been back and forth banter for months and now it seems to be escalating towards a fight. However, your character is injured from a minor, unrelated scuffle. If they fight with their enemy now it may mean sure death, but if they do not do something the situation may get worse anyway. What do they do?

957. Your character is rarely seen by human eyes. So much so that your character, and their species, have become a mythological creature in their own right. Then one day a member of the species is found by a wandering hiker. Instantly the humans flock into the habitat hoping to catch a glimpse. How does your character react?

958.   During a surprise winter storm your character has realized that the group has not collected enough food to last through the week. They can go out and look for something, risking their own life, or they can stay in the warmth of their home, hoping that the storm blows over quickly. What do they choose to do?

959.   After coming across several impressionable humans your character soon convinces them that they are a type of deity. The rouse works better than expected and they can't seem to shake these new human followers. How do they cope with the humans' unshakeable interest?

960.   While travelling their lands your character comes across a wayward human child. If they leave the child it will surely die, but your character's tribe has very strict rules against contact with humans. What does your character choose to do?

961.   Your character has decided to get itself a pet, despite the strangeness that might be perceived by others. It can go with the traditional route, like a dog or cat, or it can have something a little more outlandish. What kind of pet does your character choose?

962.   In order to make a little extra on the side your character has begun entering itself into a lot of different human sports. Others of its kind have continued to thumb their nose down at your character and eventually everything comes to a head when the group claim they will outright

disown them. Does your character try to make amends in some way?

963. Your character has managed to become violently ill in the middle of a small human neighborhood. There, they are found by a suburban family and taken to the vet of all places. How does your character show their appreciation?

964. Your character stumbles upon a slaughterhouse and witnesses all manners of cruelty. Do they decide to liberate the animals inside or do they choose to simply move along?

965. In a similar scenario suppose your character comes across an animal testing facility. Do they choose the same action then?

966. Your character has been captured by a breeder in order to pass on their desirable genetics for a profit. Does your character accept this new life or break out?

967. Suppose a breeder approaches your character and simply makes an offer to them. Do they accept?

968. After a terrifying accident your character looses a limb. This will greatly caught into their survival skills. How does your character make do?

969. Your character has ended up on the *Island of Dr. Moreau* and is set to be spliced on another species altogether. As the operation day approaches your character knows they must find some way to escape. How do they manage to get off the island?

970. Your character befriends a small child and is soon brought to class for show and tell. Unfortunately, unlike your character's new friend the other children are instantly afraid. How does your character deal with a room full of screaming children?

971. On the eve of a sacred ritual your character loses an important artifact. Without this sacred object the ritual cannot commence. Where does your character look first?

972. In the event that your character never finds this artifact, how do they break the news to the others?

973. Your character finally catches wind of a scientist who has been studying them for months. Although the scientist is relatively harmless your character knows that they have been recorded and any samples left unattended have been collected. Does your character confront the stranger?

974. After being cornered by an aggressive human your character reacts by biting them hard enough to draw blood. Although the pain itself is pretty bad it isn't long until both your character and the human realize that the saliva is poison. How does your character go on to use this new found weapon?

975. After being injured to the brink of death your character is carried off by a human and slowly nursed back to health. Before, your character would not have considered humans worthy of

your time, let alone being cared by one. Does that viewpoint still stand now that one has saved their life?

976. For some time your character has been owned by a human. Their loyalty is unquestionable but now the human needs to go on vacation and is leaving your character with a friend. How does your character cope with the new change?

977. Your character meets a mad scientist who is very eager to perform an operation. They are willing to give your character a choice in the matter: wings, fire breath, or extra scales. Does your character choose a brand new accessory despite the speculative surgery or do they quickly get out of dodge?

978. Up until now your character has been the only "pet" for their human family. However, very soon a new member shows up and they are much younger and according to the humans, "so adorable!" How does your character treat this new family member?

979. In a similar scenario imagine that your character's human family spends all of their time with this member and ignores your character. How does your character react to the lack of interest or engagement?

980. Sadly, your character's human family can no longer afford the upkeep it requires for your character. How does your character react when

they realize they're on their way to the local shelter?

981. Would that reaction be different if your character's human family could take care of them but simply did not want them anymore?

982. Your character has decided to volunteer at a local animal shelter, only it isn't for the good of the facility. Instead they plan to liberate all animals inside. How do they go about accomplishing this subversive task?

983. After committing a negative act against the humans your character is charged and sentenced to community service. What might this be?

984. Your character is found by a group of baying hound dogs. Their hunter masters are not too far behind. How does your character manage to get away?

985. After a heavy night of revelry your character wakes to find themselves inside a large cage. How might they have gotten here?

986. How might your character escape?

987. Your character tries human food for the very first time and finds out its highly addictive. They can't stop eating the stuff! The problem is that they eat so much food that they are in danger of being run out of town. How does your character manage to get their fix anyway?

988. Imagine a similar scenario in which your character tries human alcohol for the very first time. However instead of making them especially

inebriated it makes them very powerful instead. How do they best use this strange gift?

989. Your character gets into a tussle with a predator far more menacing than they. The fight is clearly in this predators favor based on brawn alone, but how does your character use is brains?

990. Your character is riding in (or driving) a vehicle for the very first time. The odd movements, the way the road passes by, and the closeness of the other drivers are all a strange experience for your character. Do they end up liking this new method of travel or will they vow never to set foot in a car again?

991. For centuries humans have enslaved your character's kind. Now your character has had enough and is going to lead a rebellion in a revolt. What action do they take first?

992. Suppose the revolt did not end well and countless soldiers, on both sides, are now gone. How does your character cope with the losses that they are the cause of?

993. Your character has been walking for miles in the middle of a dessert, finally coming across a shimmering lake of cool water...only it's a mirage. Does your character catch wind of this fabrication or do they go as far as try to drink the water that isn't there?

994. Several centuries after the apocalypse has hit, your character comes across an abandoned human

dwelling. The last existence of man is so long ago that your character has no idea what these bipedal creatures are. What kind of impressions does your character paint based off the ruins they find?

995. Your character and its people are sitting down with humans after a truce has been called. Many are calling it the "Second Thanksgiving" because a large meal is planned. What kind of foods does your character bring to the table?

996. Sadly your character comes across the body of one of its own kind. It's very clear that the hapless victim died tragically. Your character has a suspect in mind. Do they choose to take revenge or wait before jumping the gun?

997. Suppose your character blames a nearby human only to find out later that it was another member of their species. How does your character deal with their mistake?

998. In order to become the next ruler of the clan your character must fight another member to the death. The only problem is this opponent is their best friend since childhood. Does your character complete the ancient ritual anyway?

999. Your character and a human happen across each other for the very first time. Quickly a method of communication is established. What does your character say?

1000. After a terrible curse your character is turned into a human. What is the first thing they do after the change takes place?